OUR WILDLIFE WORLD

ORANGUTANS

Sheila Dalton

 Grolier

FACTS IN BRIEF

Classification of Orangutans

    Class: *Mammalia*(mammals)
    Order: *Primates*(apes, monkeys, lemurs, people)
    Family: *Pongidae*
    Genus: *Pongo*
    Species: *Pongo pygmaeus*

World distribution.   Today found only on the islands of Borneo and Sumatra in Southeast Asia.

Habitat.   Rain forests.

Distinctive physical characteristics.   Arms nearly twice as long as legs; hook-shaped hands and feet; long fur, usually reddish brown but sometimes darker; males grow fleshy cheek flaps and both sexes have throat sacs.

Habits.   Solitary; spend most of their time in trees; build nest each night to sleep in.

Diet.   Mainly fruit.

**Published originally as
"Getting to Know . . . Nature's Children."**

This series is approved and recommended by the Federation of Ontario Naturalists.

This library reinforced edition is available exclusively from:

Grolier Educational Corporation
Sherman Turnpike, Danbury, Connecticut 06816

Contents

When you look at an orangutan's thoughtful eyes, smooth forehead and small, round ears, it's easy to see why it was given a name that means "person of the forest." Of the three great apes (gorillas, chimpanzees and orangutans) orangutans are the ones whose faces look the most like ours.

The resemblance is close enough that some people believe that the orangutan was actually created by mistake! According to a Malaysian legend, two bird gods made a man and a woman, then got so excited they partied all night. The next day, they weren't feeling too well. They tried to create some more humans, but they ended up with orangutans instead.

Life in the Forest

Opposite page:

The rain forest is the perfect place for a young orangutan to play hide-and-seek.

Many years ago, orangutans lived in dense jungles from South China to Java. Today they are found in the wild only on the two islands of Borneo and Sumatra in Southeast Asia.

Orangutans make their home in tropical rain forests. Heat, humidity, floods and gales are all part of life in these forests. Vegetation is thick, and the trees are tall. As much as 20 centimetres (8 inches) of rain may fall in a day.

The orangutan doesn't mind. It is used to the heat and rain. And up in tall trees is exactly where it prefers to spend its time.

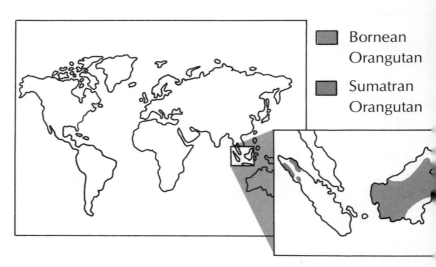

Bornean Orangutan

Sumatran Orangutan

The shaded areas on this map show where orangutans are found.

Up a Tree

Orangutans are the most arboreal of the great apes. That means they spend more of their time in trees than chimpanzees or gorillas do. They usually prefer to live near the middle of trees, but lightweight youngsters often venture up for a swing through the highest branches. Males occasionally travel on the ground, but females and babies rarely do.

An orangutan is well built for its life up in the trees. Its arms are nearly twice as long as its legs and reach down to its ankles when it stands upright. Its hands and feet are both hook-shaped — just what you need if you spend a lot of time swinging from branch to branch. As well, an orangutan's legs move as freely as its arms. In fact, it can even scratch its back with its toes!

But on the ground, the orangutan looks awkward and uncomfortable. It has to walk on the side of its feet since it cannot put them flat on the ground.

This young orangutan will grow to have an armspan of 2.4 metres (7.8 feet).

Safe and Dry

Like the other great apes, orangutans build nests up in the trees. About half an hour before sunset, which is orangutan bedtime, they pick a firm site in a fork or along a stout branch. Next, they gather lots of leafy branches and bend and twist them around one another to make a platform. Then they trample on them or pack them down with their fists, and maybe add some more broken branches and leaves to pad out the platform. To keep out the rain, they make a roof by piling leaves and twigs on overhanging branches. Or they may hold giant leaves, or big leafy branches, over their heads to act as umbrellas.

The whole task of nest making takes only about six minutes from start to finish. Most orangutans build a new nest each day, but they will return to an old one for a mid-morning nap or to sit out a rainstorm. At times, an adult male might build a nest on the ground or take a nap in a pile of leaves and twigs.

Female orangutans are very protective of their young.

Hilarious Headgear

Some scientists think the orangutan's habit of building a roof on its nest explains why it loves to put all sorts of things on its head. Others think that this behaviour may be a way of warding off stinging insects. Whatever the reason, the results can be very funny, especially when human and ape get together.

A Canadian anthropologist named Birute Galdikas lives in the rain forest of Borneo, where she often looks after orphaned baby orangutans until they are ready to cope on their own in the wild. Her young charges have been known to put anything from saucepans to potted plants on their heads. One even picked up Dr. Galdikas's pet kitten and plopped that down on its head. Talk about a furious feline!

A cosy roof of leaves.

Coat Tales

Not only do orangutans carry umbrellas, they also wear raincoats. That matted-looking mop of long reddish hair really does serve a purpose: it helps keep an orangutan's skin dry.

Actually, not all orangutans have the rusty-red fur we usually associate with them. Most do, but some of those on Borneo are maroon-tinted, and many older orangutans have chocolate-colored or almost black hair.

No matter what the shade, though, an orangutan's hair usually looks pretty messy. One reason may be that orangutans don't have anyone to groom their coats for them. Both chimpanzees and gorillas spend a lot of time grooming one another. Not so orangutans. Although females travel with their young and adolescents sometimes play together, most adults are such loners that they can go a month without seeing another orangutan.

Of course, orangutans pick dirt and insects off their skin, and mothers groom their babies. But beyond that, orangutans don't seem to notice— or care—how messy-looking their hair gets.

The Lone Ranger

There's a reason adult orangutans are such loners: they eat a lot of fruit. Fruit trees in the rain forest do not grow in clumps, but are widely scattered. If orangutans tried to stay in groups, several of them would be picking fruit off the same tree and there wouldn't be enough to go around. In fact, they'd have to find dozens of trees before everyone could be properly fed. And since orangutans are slow-moving creatures, they probably wouldn't get to enough trees in a day. An orangutan on its own, on the other hand, may only have to visit a few trees to eat its fill. In fact, if it finds a well-laden tree, one can be enough. Lone orangutans have been known to sit and feast all day in a single fruit tree.

As orangutans travel, they help the forest. The seeds of wild fruit pass through their digestive tracts and are deposited at some other place in the forest. Later, some of these seeds will grow into new fruit trees.

Dining alone again.

Food, Glorious Food

Orangutan's eat a lot because they are quite big. Although males grow only to a height of 1.5 metres (5 feet) — about the size of an average ten-year-old — they usually weigh between 50 and 90 kilograms (110-200 pounds). Females weigh somewhat more than half that and are 20 to 30 centimetres (8 to 12 inches) shorter. Both sexes eat mainly fruit.

Among other things, orangutans enjoy figs, plums and mangoes. For a bit of variety, they also snack regularly on bark, soil, leaves and insects, and treat themselves to an occasional bird's egg. But of the almost 400 varieties of food they eat, their favorite is a smelly, prickly, football-sized fruit called a durian.

Someone once said that a durian smells like a mixture of rotten eggs, onions and bad meat. Whew! Orangutans don't seem to mind the smell, though. They huff and smack their lips when munching on durians — ape-language for YUM!

A Bornean orangutan enjoys a leafy snack.

Elephants, Take Note

Orangutans have great memories. Once, an orangutan in a zoo discovered a weak spot in its cage and picked and picked at it. Finally, its keepers moved it to another cage. A year later, when it was returned to the original cage, it went right to the weak spot and started picking at it again.

Having a good memory helps the orangutan survive in the rain forest. Not only are the fruit trees there small and scattered, but some only produce fruit once every two or three years. And even then, the fruits don't ripen all at the same time. Without a good memory for time and place, orangutans could wear themselves out searching for food, and still they might not find enough. As it is, however, adult orangutans seem able to carry a map of their territory in their head, showing where each type of fruit grows — and when it will ripen.

So even though a typical orangutan brain is only one-third the size of yours, these hairy beasts are far from dumb.

Opposite page: Orangutans don't drink much— sometimes they sip dew off plants or scoop out water trapped in holes in trees with their hands.

Good Senses

Not only are they smart, orangutans have excellent hearing and color vision. Because they don't have to fear many predators, they use their small, rounded ears mostly to listen for the calls of other orangutans. Good eyesight is helpful in finding fruit.

Since an orangutan sleeps for up to twelve hours at night, it doesn't need especially good night vision. And because it finds its food by memory and sight, it doesn't need (or have) a well-developed sense of smell. No wonder the rotten-smelling durian doesn't bother it at all!

An orangutan on the alert.

Tough Times

Life can look pretty easy for orangutans in the wild. They move slowly and rest a lot. In fact, an orangutan can spend over half a day napping.

But orangutans have their share of problems. They don't have to worry much about predators, but they suffer from broken bones and from fleas, ticks and other parasites. And they can catch human diseases such as pneumonia, malaria and polio.

Human beings are the orangutan's biggest problem. Sometimes people kill female orangutans so that they can capture their babies and sell them as pets or zoo animals. Logging and farming pose a threat, too; if the rain forest is cut down, the orangutan will have nowhere to live.

Solutions are being found, though. The governments of Borneo and Sumatra have made it illegal to capture or kill orangutans. And, all over the world, people are banding together to help save the rain forests.

"Wake me when it's time for dinner."

Face to Face

Many people think the world would be a poorer place without the "person of the forest." One of the many things that make the orangutan unique is its expressive face. Although they look like one another at first glance, it is really quite easy to tell individual orangutans apart. Their facial features, like ours, can vary a lot — more than those of the other great apes.

Bornean and Sumatran orangutans have slightly different faces. The Sumatran orangutan has a long, oval face. The Bornean's is thicker and broader. Both types have facial hair, but the Sumatran male grows a much fuller beard and mustache than the Bornean male.

There is another difference. Adult males of both types have big, fat cheeks — but the Bornean's grow so big, he can barely see around them!

It's hard to believe, but in the matter of cheek flaps, this Sumatran orangutan is outdone by his Bornean cousin.

Flap, Flap, I Love You

Scientists are not sure why male orangutans develop such fat faces, but they think those fleshy flaps might actually make a male more attractive to females that are ready to mate. Fat cheeks might also be a handy source of nourishment. When food is scarce, the orangutan's body could possibly use the fat stored in its cheeks to survive until more tasty fare becomes available.

Both males and females develop throat sacs that serve much the same purpose as the amplifier on your stereo, making the orangutan's calls louder. Males have particularly impressive pouches and can blow them up like giant balloons when they want to let the world know they're around.

A thoughtful moment.

The Long Call

When a male orangutan blows up his throat pouch and lets rip, he is making what is known as the "long call." This tremendous sound can last anywhere from two to four minutes. It usually starts with a low rumble, turns into a noise like a trumpeting elephant, then ends with long sighs. Some people who have heard it say the whole thing sounds like one huge burp! However you describe it, it is loud enough to be heard from a kilometre or so (over half a mile) away.

The long call is used mainly to warn other males to stay out of an orangutan's territory, but it comes in handy for attracting females, too. It is also useful for locating other orangutans in the forest. Although they are solitary, orangutans like to keep tabs on one another's whereabouts.

Orangutans make a dozen or more other sounds, including a warning "bark." And females use a particular call described as a "kiss-squeak" to express annoyance with a male's unwelcome attentions.

"Don't come any closer!"

Enter at Your Own Risk

Many male orangutans claim a territory of about 5 square kilometres (2 square miles). Several females usually live within this area on overlapping home ranges of about 100 hectares (250 acres) each. Females limit their movement to an area just big enough to feed themselves and their offspring. Males travel farther afield, looking for mates in addition to food.

A male uses the long call to protect his territory, and if that doesn't work, he indulges in a show of strength called a display. He does this by ripping branches from trees and throwing them on the ground or shaking them furiously. He also inflates his throat pouch and makes threatening grunting noises.

When two adult males meet, they often display, but they seldom fight. The male who is trespassing on the other's territory usually gives in fairly soon. If they do fight, it will likely be over a female who is ready to mate.

Despite their threatening appearance, male orangutans rarely fight.

Getting Together

A female orangutan can mate when she is 7 years old, but often she will wait until she is 10 or 11 to take a partner. After she has a baby, she will not mate again until the largest part of child-rearing is over. This takes at least four years and sometimes it may be eight or nine years before the female mates again. For this reason, and since the female almost always has only one baby at a time, the orangutan population grows slowly.

A male can mate when he is 10, but he often has to wait. Females seem to prefer bigger males, between 12 and 15 years old. These are the males who have fought for and won their own territory. They are the strongest males around, and so should father the strongest, healthiest offspring.

"Mom, listen to how loud I can yell!"

Hang On There, Baby

Nine months after mating, the female gives birth in her nest in a tree. The newborn orangutan weighs between one and two kilograms (two and four pounds) and is usually covered with orange fur. Its brown face has light areas around the eyes and mouth, which will darken as it grows older.

The new mother stays in the nest with her baby for at least a week, until it is old enough to travel. As soon as it can hang on tightly to her fur, she's on the move again. Then Junior is in for a safe but bumpy ride, as mother and baby swing through the trees together.

Sometimes it's exhausting being a young orangutan.

Super Mom

Female orangutans make very good mothers. They protect their babies from danger and hug and snuggle, just as your mom did when you were little. Sometimes they play games, like tickle-your-toes and hide-and-seek, with their young.

Many young orangutans cling to their mother almost continually until they are around a year and a half old. They drink her milk, and they ride on her body and share her nest for at least three years, and sometimes they stay with her for as many as six or seven years. A mother orangutan cleans her baby's fur and keeps its fingernails short with her teeth. She also washes it with rain water.

It's difficult to believe that this nearly naked 6-week-old orangutan will one day be as large and hairy as its mother.

Acting Like A Baby

In some ways, baby orangutans are a lot like human babies. They cry when they are hungry or uncomfortable. They seek affection from Mom by climbing into her lap or nuzzling and snuggling up to her. They also have a wide range of emotions. They get sad, happy and angry. Once, a mother orangutan was a bit slow to share a mango with her little one. The baby threw a temper tantrum — squealing and jumping up and down in rage. Mom ignored the racket for a while, then calmly handed her offspring a slice as if nothing unusual had happened.

Compared with human babies, however, baby orangutans show little interest in language or tools. In fact, they show little interest in anything but food!

"Which one should I eat first?"

Lessons from Mom

The young orangutan learns how to take care of itself slowly and steadily. First, it figures out what's good to eat — and what's not — by watching Mom. Mom plays a more active role when it comes to climbing and walking. She pushes her youngster out on branches, or leaves it alone on the ground, so that it has no choice but to learn how to get around on its own.

By the time they are four, most orangutan youngsters can select their own food, swing through the trees on their own and make nests. They still choose to sleep with Mom at night, but they are getting more and more able to take care of themselves.

Going It Alone

When its mother has a new baby, the young orangutan finds itself pushed out of the family nest. At first, it doesn't like this at all! It tries to get back in, and Mom may have to smack and even bite it before it will go away and build its own nest.

For a while, the youngster hangs around its mother and the new baby during the day and nests close to them at night. It may even entertain the new baby now and then with games of peek-a-boo. Then, one day, it may meet up with some other adolescent orangutans and wander off with them — the first step to a life on its own.

With luck, and if its habitat is not destroyed, the young orangutan can look forward to anywhere from 40 to 60 years of swinging through the rain forest.

Words to Know

Ape   Group of animals that includes gorillas, chimpanzees, orangutans, gibbons and siamangs. The first three are known as the great apes.

Arboreal   That lives in trees.

Display   A noisy performance a male orangutan puts on to scare away other males.

Durian   A foul-smelling but pleasant-tasting fruit particularly favored by orangutans.

Groom   To clean or brush, especially hair.

Home range   Area through which an animal moves in search of food.

Long call   Name given to particularly loud call made by male orangutans and lasting two to four minutes.

Parasite   Organism that grows and feeds on the body of another. Fleas and ticks are parasites.

Rain forest   Densely forested area that receives over 250 centimeters (100 inches) of rain a year.

Territory   Area that an animal or a group of animals lives in and often defends from other animals of the same kind.

INDEX

Cover Photo: Dede Gilman (Unicorn Stock Photos)

Photo Credits: Bill Ivy, pages 4, 24, 36; Kjell B. Sandved, pages 7, 12; Evelyn Gallardo, page 8; Douglas T. Cheeseman, Jr., page 11; Louie Bunde (Unicorn Stock Photos), pages 15, 32; Tom McHugh (Photo Researchers, Inc.), page 16, 27, 40; Boyd Norton, page 19, 44; Nancy Adams, pages 20, 23; Four By Five, pages 28, 43; Alice Taylor (Photo Researchers, Inc.), page 31; Shostal Associates, page 35; Nancy Staley, pages 38, 39.

DATE DUE